Copyright

All rights reserved. No part of this workbook may be reproduced or transmitted in any form or by any means electronic or mechanical, including photocopying, recording, or by any information or retrieval system, without permission from the author, except for the inclusion of brief quotations in a review.

© Copyright 2015 by David Denniston. All rights reserved. 3rd edition 2015.

Published in the United States of America.

About the Author

Dave Denniston, CFA is a financial advisor and author working with physicians of all ages and enjoys particularly focusing on residents and fellows.

In working with clients for over 10 years, he has seen most every situation imaginable. The one common theme he found that separates the successful and thriving clients is one thing- debt.

His drive and passion to see every doctor's financial situation become debt-free has led him to write this workbook.

His drive to help doctors came from the birth of his youngest child, Evangeline. She is his family's little miracle baby born in May 2012 four months prematurely at a weight of 12.5 oz (3.5 oz short of 1 pound!). As they were in the NICU for nearly five months, he had the opportunity to get to know many residents and fellows and listen to what they go through. He decided from then on that he was on a mission to help out every possible resident or fellow. It became quickly evident that the best way to do that was to write, speak, and meet with people individually to council with them on their financial situation.

He is an expert in a number of financial planning topics including debt reduction, 457 DCs, 403bs, and other retirement plans, asset allocation (where to invest), disability income insurance, life insurance, annuities, college planning, stock awards and options, and much more.

He has written other workbooks on a variety of subjects that are available for sale on Amazon.com including- *The Tax Reduction Prescription Workbook for Physicians*, *The Insurance Guide for Doctors*, and his "big book" *The Freedom Formula for Physicians: A Prescription for First Class Financial Health for Doctors*. He is planning to write at least 1 "big book" a year on other subjects related to physicians. His latest project a how-to guide for residents and fellows on investments, insurance, & contracts.

He resides in Bloomington, MN with his wife of more than a decade, Cyrena, and his two children, Gabby and Evangeline.

For regular videos updates and newsletters on a variety of financial subjects, check out his website at www.daviddenniston.com/physicians or his Podcast at www.DoctorFreedomPodcast.com.

Lastly, make sure to check out the very last page of this workbook for the MOST INCREDIBLE offer ever!

Summary

Perhaps, you are a young physician just out of medical school. No more tests or studying, you've just landed your feet!

Or maybe you are now in your residency or fellowship and making a little bit of dough. You're starting to think about the future.

Now what?

According to the American medical School Association[1], 86% of medical school graduate carry educational debt and that the median debt burden is $119,000 for public school graduates and nearly $150,000 for private school graduates.

Frankly, this sounds too low to me. I see many young physicians with $200,000, $300,000, or even $400,000 in school debt.

I believe that too many of us have too much debt, and that I can help. I am on a mission to reduce, demolish, destroy, and obliterate your debt.

Think about this question for a moment….

What would your life be like if you did not have any more debt?

Would you retire earlier? Would you take more vacations? Would you give more gifts to your children? Would you give more money to a charitable cause?

I am here today to give you some weapons to vanquish this beast. I will equip you with some tools to assist you in getting on the winding pathway towards financial freedom.

Take the next step- complete this workbook. Use this tool to reflect, strategize, and project yourself in the future. Revisit it on an annual basis.

If you would like any additional support and to learn more about how I can serve you, please feel free to contact me anytime at dave@daviddenniston.com or call me at (800) 548-1890.

Let's take this journey together and get you on the path to financial freedom.

Warm Regards,

OVERVIEW

Define Your Financial Reality & Goals

In order to be debt free, you must know where you are heading. You know how hard it is to get someplace when you don't have a roadmap?

I have certainly gotten lost a few times when I don't know where I am going. Thank goodness for GPS in cell phones today!

Let's work together on defining your financial reality and understanding the destination of where you want to go. Let's design a roadmap for your path to the ultimate destination: financial freedom. After all, you can't plan a trip if you don't know **when** you are going as well as **where** you are going.

In this workbook, we are going to address the following:

- Preparing Your Net Worth Statement. Understanding "producing" assets versus "non-producing" assets.
- Understanding your liabilities
- Define Your Roadmap Debt "Goals"
- How to Determine Importance & Pay-Off Decisions
- What Am I Spending Monthly & Where can I improve?

The exercises in this module are incredibly important in building the cornerstone of your debt reduction plan. For many of us, this can be difficult to look at. Sometimes, we need a guiding hand. <u>Don't hesitate to ask for help if you find you are procrastinating or just can't stand looking at the data on your own.</u>

STEP One | Preparing Your Net Worth Statement- Assets

First, let's understand the difference between producing assets and nonproducing assets.

- **Producing Assets.** Producing assets are investments that are made for the sole purpose of trying to increase your net worth. They usually produce capital gains, dividends, income, or are relatively easy to sell. This includes your accounts at the bank, your investment accounts, insurance contracts, precious metals, and rental real estate.

- **Nonproducing assets.** Meanwhile, nonproducing assets are purchased primarily for pleasure and use. They usually do not produce income and can be very difficult to sell.

This category includes your home (after all, you have to live somewhere!), your second home/cabin, cars, boats, artwork, and hobby collections (e.g., antiques, stamps, etc.).

Next, gather the data you will need for all of your assets. (We'll cover liabilities in step two, but feel free to get those statements as well)

1.1 Action Step: Gather together the data that you will need for all of your assets. (We'll cover liabilities in step two, but feel free to get those statements as well).

Inventory of producing assets. First, make an inventory of all your producing assets. Get all bank statements (checking/savings/money market/ CDs), investment statements (brokerage account, stocks, bonds, 401(K), 457 DC, 403b, etc), life & long-term care insurance policies, and information regarding any rental properties or investment real estate. Use Zillow.com or the last property tax valuation to get an approximation of real estate values.

Inventory of non-producing assets. Secondly, make an inventory of all your non-producing assets as discussed above.

Utilize the chart below to help yourself get organized. I've included a small sample for your review.

Asset Description	Asset Category	Company	Account #	Ownership	Value	Availability
IRA FBO David	Retirement	Investors Capital	6BB-000000	David	$ 50,000	5/12/2041
Checking	Liquid	Wells Fargo	1234567	Joint	$ 30,000	Now
Savings	Liquid	Wells Fargo	1234568	Joint	$ 5,000	Now
Variable Annuity	Retirement	Transamerica	123456LBT	Joint	$100,000	1/1/2016
Joint Brokerage	Non-Qualified	Investors Capital	6BB-000001	Joint	$ 15,000	Now
Rental Property	Non-Qualified	n/a	n/a	Joint	$200,000	Not Liquid

A quick primer on a few of these columns...

Asset category is divided into three possibilities: Liquid, Non-Qualified, and Retirement. **Try to write them down as sorted by the asset category. Liquid assets first, then non-qualified, and then retirement. Print out an additional sheet if needed.**

- **Liquid assets.** Liquid assets are anything at the bank- Checking, Savings, Money Market, and CDs.

- **Non-qualified assets.** Non-qualified assets are assets that you could liquidate without any tremendous tax penalty and don't have restrictions placed on them by the government. This commonly includes brokerage accounts, stock awards and options, and real estate investments.

- **Retirements assets.** Retirement assets are assets that give you a tax advantage due to a tax deduction or tax deferral. This commonly includes 401(k), 457 DC, 403b, IRA, Roth IRA, annuities, and cash value life insurance.

Make sure to find out if your life insurance policy has a cash value. This usually applies to universal life, whole life, and variable life policies. Term insurance policies do not have a cash value and should not be included as an asset.

Another column on the chart is **availability**. This is the ability to withdraw the funds without worrying about penalties. For example, you cannot withdraw funds from IRAs or 401(k)s until you are 59.5 years old or there is an early withdrawal penalty of 10%. Some annuities have surrender penalties on them for varying terms- some are 4 years, others are 7 years, or even 10 years.

Producing Assets

Asset Description	Asset Category	Company	Ownership	Account Number	Value	Availability

For more information, go to www.daviddenniston.com/physicians or www.DoctorFreedomPodcast.com.
For questions, e-mail: dave@daviddenniston.com
Or call 800-548-1820

Non-Producing Assets

Asset Description	Where is It?	Ownership	Value

STEP two | Preparing Your Net Worth Statement- Liabilities

Next, let's discuss liabilities. These are the debts and loans that we are looking to eliminate! Before we figure out how to get rid of these, first we need to identify the loans and make an inventory of them. I really believe that being organized is more than half the battle. After getting this done, you will be well on your way!

We are going to need the following information about your liabilities: Description, Company, Principal Owed, Interest Rate, Maturity Date, Minimum Payment, Current Payment, Loan Type (House, Consumer, or Business), Fixed versus Variable, and if variable, when it changes.

To be clearer about what we are looking for, here are a few pointers:

- If you have a credit card that you pay off monthly and does <u>not</u> have a balance that continues, you don't need to include it here.

- We include minimum payment versus current payment because some folks pay more than the minimum and we want to make sure to understand the difference. Perhaps, you could pay less to some liabilities and more to others.

- If you own <u>rental homes</u>, consider that <u>Business Debt</u> rather than House debt. 'House debt' is meant to show the tax deductible debt on your primary residence. Likewise, we consider 401k loans, life insurance loans, and student loans 'consumer debt'.

- *The reason why we consider student loans as 'consumer debt' is because they stop becoming tax deductible once your income reaches a certain level. Currently, that is <u>$65,000</u> if you are single or <u>$130,000</u> if you are married.*

- Lastly, to understand whether a loan is fixed versus variable- the main question to ask is if the interest rate could change sometime in the future. Home equity lines of credit (HELOC), adjustable rate mortgages (ARMs), credit cards, and business lines of credit are all common examples of variable loans.

The Retired Surgeon

He has a beautiful home overlooking the sparking Pacific Ocean. He loves to fish and boat and kayak. Every time I get together with he and his wife, I know they are going to ask me one question. Just one…

Here's the question they ask…

"Are we going to have enough money to last for the rest of our lives?"

Tough question, right! What's the answer? Let me tell you a little bit more about him.

He once wrote me a letter that said,

"Physicians are notorious for being poor investors. While a medical student, there were no courses to guide us when we started to make money as a physician. University faculty seemed to abhor the discussion. As soon as I was making money, I paid off my medical school debts and started to save and invested in stocks."

He goes on and on..

"One of the things that [Judy] and I have tried to do is limit our debt. We paid off our home within 10 years, paid cash for cars, boats, etc, and have never carried a credit card debt."

Ladies and gentleman, with this client, I am not concerned with him EVER running out of money.

Why?

It's because he understood one basic principle- debt sucks!

Who can agree with me here?

Due to the extremely high level of student debt that most physicians hold, many are eligible for several types of forbearance programs and debt-reduction programs. The difficulty lies in choosing among them all.

Truly, physicians have a wonderful opportunity to enroll in debt forgiveness programs. Later on, we'll ask you to think about and explore whether a loan forgiveness program may make sense for you. Here are a few factors that you may want to consider when looking over the possibilities:

- **Does this cover my field of practice?**
- **Do you specify a specific loan or can you get forgiveness on multiple loans?**
- **Is this an employer or a state funded program?**
- **Are the benefits taxable or not?**
- **What is the length of the commitment?**
- **Does the employer or the state pay down the loan each year or do they wait until the end of the commitment?**

Let's look at a couple of examples of some debt forgiveness programs…

The Public Service Loan Forgiveness Program (PSLF)

The most common debt program that physicians look into is the 10-Year Public Loan Forgiveness program.

This is sponsored by the Federal Government and can cover virtually any field of practice. You don't have to specify a specific loan because it can cover all of your loans (assuming they have been Stafford, Perkins, and other federally backed programs). The benefits are currently not taxable, but this could change in the future.

As the name mentions, it is a 10 year program. The federal government will not forgive the balance until the end of the program.

HOW THE 10-YEAR PROGRAM WORKS

Here's how it works…

While you are employed full-time for a public service organization, you must make 120 on-time, full monthly payments (INCLUDES residency/fellowship).

Think about this for a minute- this is just seven years out of residency or maybe only three, four, or five years out of fellowship!

Note that if you have FFEEL and/or Perkins loans, you need to consolidate them into a Direct Consolidation Loan to take advantage of the program.

Qualifying employment is any employment with a federal, state, or local government agency OR a non-profit that has a 501c3 status. Also, this includes certain non-profits that aren't 501c3s.

LET ME EMPHASIZE THIS STRONGLY- if you are employed by a hospital that has a non-profit 501c3 status- you are probably eligible for this program!

Make sure to be aware whether the arm that you are working for is a non-profit or for-profit. Some non-profit hospitals can have a for-profit subsidiary for tax reasons.

Note that your monthly payments are substantially lower while in residency and fellowship. We will go through some examples later for after residency and fellowship.

Think about this for a minute….

If you are in residency for three years, you will only have seven years remaining on payments.

Meanwhile if you have a fellowship for three years in addition to three years of residency, you only have four years remaining on payments!

The bottom line is to make sure you to enroll AS SOON AS POSSIBLE while you are in residency and fellowship!

Here's how it works…

If you have FFEEL and/or Perkins loans, you need to consolidate them into a direct consolidation loan to take advantage of the program. This is a process will take one to three months to complete depending upon your situation.

HOW REPAYMENT WORKS

As you complete the direct consolidation loan, you must pick a repayment program. The four most common programs are the Income-Based Repayment (IBR) Plan, Pay-As-You-Earn (PER), Plan, the Income-Contingent Repayment (ICR) Plan, and the 10-Year Standard Repayment Plan.

In this book, we focus on IBR and PER as they require lower payments in residency and fellowship which can lead to greater debt forgiveness.

Next, you start to make on-time monthly payments for the ensuing 120 months.

Make sure EVERY YEAR to complete, with your employer's certification, the Employment Certification form or whenever you change jobs.

Submit the completed form to FedLoan Servicing (PHEAA), the PSLF servicer, following the instructions on the form.

FedLoan Servicing (PHEAA) will review your Employment Certification form, ensure that it is complete, and based on the information provided by your employer, determine whether your employment is qualifying employment for the PSLF Program.

DIFFERENCE BETWEEN INCOME-BASED REPAYMENT & PAY-AS-YOU-EARN REPAYMENT PLANS

The most common program is the Income-Based Repayment (IBR). The second more recent program is the Pay-As-You Earn Repayment (PER or PAYE).

IBR and PER both accomplish the same goal, minimizing your student debt payments while in residency/fellowship and then paying back your student loans at a higher rate once you are making more dough.

REQUIREMENTS

Note that IBR and PER both require a "partial financial hardship". This means in comparing to federal student loan under a 10-year Standard Repayment Plan is HIGHER than under IBR or PER.

COMMITMENT

The commitment for IBR will a monthly payment of 15% of discretionary income whereas under PER the commitment will only 10% of discretionary income. Note that discretionary income has a very specific definition- your income minus poverty guidelines published by the government.

ADJUSTMENTS

They will ask questions about your household- i.e. spouse, spousal school loans, kids, etc as those effect the poverty guidelines. How do they determine your income? By looking at your tax return!

This is an important distinction because the government is purely looking at your "adjusted gross income". This means that they are taking a snapshot of your income AFTER pre-tax deductions for 401k/403b contributions, AFTER pre-tax deductions for health-savings accounts, and AFTER deductions for any active business losses.

5 Steps To Get Out of Debt Action Guide for Physicians

Also, this means that if you ended your residency/fellowship in June and started your first contract in July that you would likely not have to start having higher payments UNTIL the following year. For example, if you finished your residency in June 2013- your higher payments will not take effect until past January 2014.

However, the payments DO NOT take into consideration your overall student load debt nor your age nor whether you have a car loan, mortgage, etc. The student debt load is a particularly interesting as we explore debt forgiveness programs.

Below is a table that I composed by entering information on the calculators at studentaid.ed.gov.

Note that I assumed that this person is married, has no kids, no spousal school loans, that the original loans were $20,000 to $30,000 below the current loan amount, and that the loans carry an interest rate of 6.8%.

While you could like easily qualify for IBR while in residency, the calculator on the website doesn't allow me to calculate the payment at a $200,000 income level, $150,000 loan amount for IBR.

However, we could safely assume that the payment should be $2,216/month given the example below because the monthly payment fluctuates with compensation, but not with the loan amount.

Compensation	Loan Amount	IBR	PER
$150,000	$150,000	$1,591/mo	$1,061/mo
$150,000	$250,000	$1,591/mo	$1,061/mo
$200,000	$150,000	*Does not qualify	$1,478/mo
$200,000	$250,000	$2,216/mo	$1,478/mo

Note the tremendous difference between IBR and PER- over $500/month at the $150,000 compensation level and over $700/month at the $200,000 compensation level. See how the IBR or PER amount does NOT change as the loan amount goes up? This is because it is primarily dependent on income.

There is one big caveat between the two programs. To qualify for PER, you could not have any current student debt that originated before 2007.

For more information, go to www.daviddenniston.com/physicians or www.DoctorFreedomPodcast.com.
For questions, e-mail: dave@daviddenniston.com
Or call 800-548-1820

5 Steps To Get Out of Debt Action Guide for Physicians

How does all of this tie in with loan forgiveness programs? Let's take a look at an example where two physicians, Dr. Smith and Dr. Jones, who started PSLF at the very start of residency. They each had an equal amount of student debt coming out of medical school.

Dr. Smith has been in residency for three years, has made 36 payments towards PSLF, and went right into practice. He is making $150,000 per year.

Meanwhile, Dr. Jones has also been in residency for three years, has made 36 payments towards PSLF, and also just entered into practice. He is now making $200,000 per year.

Let's examine the difference of what would happen if each of them enrolled in IBR or PER at the start of residency.

The table below adds up the monthly payments from the previous example and multiplies them over seven years. There is no increase in salary. I'm keeping it simple and flat. The lifetime payments in the table are the combination of interest AND principal over those seven years.

Compensation	Loan Amount	IBR- Lifetime	PER- Lifetime
$150,000	$150,000	$133,644	$89,124
$150,000	$250,000	$133,644	$89,124
$200,000	$150,000	*Does not qualify	$124,152
$200,000	$250,000	$186,144	$124,152

At the end of the seven years (assuming continued non-profit employment), the remaining portion of their debt would be forgiven.

For example with $250,000 of loans and $150,000 worth of compensation, after seven years in practice you will have paid about $90,000 in PER relative to about $130,000 in IBR assuming your taxable income is $150,000.

After Dr. Smith completes 84 remaining payments now that he is in practice, this would be approximately $225,000 worth of forgiveness with IBR versus $265,000 of forgiveness with PER.

This is why PER is superior to IBR when you tie in the student debt forgiveness programs with them.

Additionally, the higher your loans, the more beneficial it will be to be enrolled in PER. Let's say that you have $250,000 in student loans.

Consider this, at an interest rate of 6.8%, you are accruing interest of about $17,000/annually or $1,416/month. With PER, you would have been paying $1,478/month- barely taping into principal.

Then, over 7 years, you will have paid about $124,000 and will have debt forgiveness of almost $250,000 of principal- and likely tax-free!

Giving up this gift is the tax equivalent of almost $360,000 or $51,000/year over 7 years assuming a 30% tax bracket.

Even with IBR, you would still have debt forgiveness of nearly $200,000 or the approximate tax equivalent of $285,000.

Either is wonderful, but PER is better for debt forgiveness purposes!

Remember- like we mentioned earlier, to qualify for PER, you must have student debt that originated after October 2007. This will likely start effecting residents and fellows that started in 2012 and even more so over the next few years.

ATTENTION: YOUNG PHYSICIANS WHO WANT TO GROW THEIR FAMILY

Tick... tick... tick.... The biological clock may be ticking.

I was meeting with a wonderful couple the other day, two neurologists. They are just transitioning into practice and they are so excited!

Their income is going to be awesome and they'll have so much cash flow they won't know what to do with it. Okay, okay, I'm sure they'll figure out some ways to spend that dough. =-)

In reviewing over their financial situation, we came to the tough question of debt.

He has 300k+ in medical school debt and she has 200k+ in medical school debt.

Here they are- gone through undergrad, gone through medical school, gone through residency, and now gone through fellowship- in their mid 30's and left with a mountain of debt.

Time is running out! Tick... tick... tick... Her biological clock is ticking and they want to start a family.

They both have enrolled into IBR and have been minimizing their payments, yet checking off the days towards PSLF allowing them to be debt free.

However, when we talked about their future plans and their family. I wondered whether or not this was the right move.

You see, after having their first kiddo, she is mulling over cutting back down on work to half-time, a 0.5.

I thought that was great and wonderful, but it doesn't work for IBR & PSLF!

PSLF requires that you work FULL-TIME to get your credit for the year. On studentaid.ed.gov they say, *"You are generally considered to work full-time if you meet your employer's definition of full-time or work at least 30 hours per week, whichever is greater.*

If you are employed in more than one qualifying part-time job at the same time, you may meet the full-time employment requirement if you work a combined average of at least 30 hours per week with your employers."

This is very interesting- you have to meet your employer's definition of full-time OR at least 30 hours per week, whichever is **GREATER**.

In this case, half-time at 20 hours or 25 hours per week isn't going to cut it. Those years that she takes to still work BUT not full-time and raise her family will NOT qualify!

Thus, I was highly pushing them towards having the husband neurologist's loans work towards IBR/PSLF as planned. After all, we are talking about 300k+ in potential forgiveness!

However, we need to change it up for the wife neurologist's loans. I emphasized that we should refinance her loans through SoFi, DRB, or another loan consolidator.

I ended up listing off five different reasons why I thought this was important:

1) That she was considering going half-time
2) This ensures no matter what happens with the government & PSLF, that about half of their loans are in their power and thus can be erased on their terms
3) It immediately lowers the interest rate on her loans
4) It allows her once they have their debts paid off to have the freedom to quit altogether and stay home with the kids if she wishes
5) This makes an unknown variable a known variable that will make it easier to plan

You should have seen the look they gave me.

Their noses crinkled, eyes blank, and heads dipped downward. The room was very quiet.

They struggled with the idea and to be honest, have yet to implement it.

I worry about them and can audibly hear the biological clock going going tick…. tick… tick…

WHAT CAN WE CONCLUDE FROM IBR VS. PER?

If you are working for a **non-profit** entity, PER is probably a better option unless you do not qualify due to the origination of your student debt. IBR will still be a fine choice.

I would strongly suggest NOT to put extra payments towards your debts if you are enrolled in the 10 Year Public Loan Forgiveness Program unless you think you may not be ready to make a 10 year commitment to staying in the non-profit community.

If you are currently working for a **non-profit** and are considering **transitioning to a for-profit** practice after residency, IBR would be my recommendation. Keep in mind that you can make extra payments beyond the minimum that IBR requires to pay it off sooner once you are in practice.

Two Doctors- Married…. But Separated

What if you are married? Is there a different strategy?

Let me take you back a few years…

It's the happiest day of your life! Your wedding day… Best. Day. Ever.

Smiles, hugs, the white gown, the champagne, the first dance, the cake, and the limo. Laughter peels through the air. Fleeting memories of vows and eager faces, music hanging in the air. Although, you could do without the bit of the mother-in-law drama!

You're a physician who is married to another physician. There is no doubt, the two of you have an incredibly bright future ahead of you. After all, you're going to be making almost $400,000 combined!

You're just getting through the final year of your residency. Practice is just ahead! You'll finally be able to buy a house, go on vacations, and not be scraping by on a champion's diet of apples, oranges, and top ramen.

Then it hits you like you just ran into a brick wall- $500,000 of medical school debt…. How the heck are you ever going to get out of that debt?

Is it going to take 20 years? 30 years?

You've enrolled in the Public Service Loan Forgiveness Program (PSLF) and you think it may only take another 8 years if you are lucky. However, the payments are going to be killer in another year- almost $5,000 a month between the two of you! That will kill the hopes to save for a home quickly. How the heck could you afford it?

Then, you meet some crazy financial guy that tells you that you need to get separated…

SAY WHAT?

We just got married and now we have to get separated?

WHY TWO MARRIED PHYSICIANS SHOULD FILE MARRIED FILING SEPARATELY

Okay, I don't mean that these two physicians have to get separated legally, but instead be married filing separately on THEIR TAXES.

The two currently do not have to be one and the same. It is a choice!

I had this same situation happen to me recently when two physician clients came into my office to explore their options on re-paying their debts.

DISCLAIMER: These are two physicians who are working in a hospital setting, thus under a non-profit. Remember, in order to qualify for loan forgiveness under PSLF, you have to work for a non-profit or a government entity.

We explored the differences between married filing jointly versus married filing separately. I was astounded by the results.

Below are three tables showing several scenarios we ran to show how married filing separately versus married filing jointly can affect your payments, and thus the potential loan forgiveness.

In this real-life scenario, the wife is now in practice- she transitioned in July of 2014. He is two years behind and will be transitioning to practice in July of 2016.

Keep in mind that the IBR payment changes AFTER you report your income- let's say by May of each year. For simplification purposes, we will assume it happens in January of each calendar year.

The wife- Dr. Giselle Smith- $110,000 in eligible student debt.

Scenario	Income	IBR Payment
Single	$55,000	$469/mo
Married Filing Jointly/ One Still In Residency, Other In Practice	$240,000	$726/mo
Married Filing Jointly/	$370,000	$1,100/mo

5 Steps To Get Out of Debt Action Guide for Physicians

Both In Practice		
Married Filing Separately (Only Her Income)- Transition Year	$120,000	$328/mo
Married Filing Separately (Only Her Income)- Fully In Practice	$185,000	$537/mo

The husband- Dr. Tom Smith- $315,000 in eligible student debt.

Scenario	Income	IBR Payment
Single	$53,000	$444/mo
Married Filing Jointly/ One Still In Residency, Other In Practice	$240,000	$2,002/mo
Married Filing Jointly/ Both In Practice	$370,000	$3,220/mo
Married Filing Separately (Only His Income in Residency)	$55,000	$349/mo
Married Filing Separately (Only His Income)- Transition Year	$120,000	$953/mo
Married Filing Separately (Only Her Income)- Fully In Practice	$185,000	$1,557/mo

Combined- Husband and Wife Together

5 Steps To Get Out of Debt Action Guide for Physicians

Scenario	IBR Payment- Married Filing Jointly	IBR Payment- Married Filing Separately
Year 1- She is Fully In Practice (transition year income was previous year), He is full year in residency	$2,084/mo	$677/mo
Year 2- She is fully in practice, he is full year in residency	$2,728/mo	$886/mo
Year 3- she is fully in practice, he is in transition year	$3,074/mo	$1,490/mo
Year 4 & beyond- both are fully in practice	$4,320/mo	$2,094/mo
TOTAL PAYMENTS IN 4 YEARS	$146,472	$61,764
DIFFERENCE	$84,080	

We could go on and on, but check it out- you could be saving yourself literally HUNDREDS OF THOUSANDS of dollars IF your debts get forgiven through PSLF PLUS being married filing separately.

Keep in mind to look at this decision holistically before jumping in the pool and filing this way. There are real-world tax consequences to this decision when you file for taxes as married filing separately versus married filing jointly.

In this particular instance, the difference was minimal- only about $2,000 per year in combined federal and state income taxes. It made far more of an impact on their debt reduction to go for it, rather than take the cash flow hit.

Make sure to discuss any potential tax impact with your advisors so that you fully understand the consequences.

Other Debt Forgiveness Programs

State Sponsored Debt Forgiveness Programs

Besides, PSLF, there are some really exciting opportunities offered in every state.

Make sure to check out state sponsored programs at: https://services.aamc.org/fed_loan_pub/.

As of the time of this writing (October 2015), there were over 71 different programs available across the country!

Here is an example of a current program in Minnesota...

Minnesota Urban Physician Loan Forgiveness Program

Who? Applicants are primary care medical residents, which include Family Practice, Obstetrics and Gynecology, Pediatrics, Internal Medicine and Psychiatry. You would apply July 1 to December 1 while completing medical residency training.

Requirements. Following completing of the residency, the participant must plan to practice for at least 30 hours per week, for at least 45 weeks per year, for a minimum of three years in an underserved urban community.

The Nitty Gritty Payment Details. The state will re-pay up to $25,000 per year of service, not to exceed $100,000 or the balance of the designated loan, whichever is less.

Tax Consequences. These payments are exempt from state and federal income taxes. $25,000 is the taxable equivalent of $35,700 (assuming a 30% tax bracket).

Time Commitment. You must serve at least three years or otherwise must repay plus interest what they paid towards your loan.

Here's another example of another state forgiveness program...

Oregon Partnership State Loan Repayment (SLRP)

Who? Applicants are primary care medical physicians and psychologists (among other non-physician positions).

Requirements. Must be a US Citizen. The application period is normally open during October and November each year and awards are made in December.

The Nitty Gritty Payment Details. Qualifying providers can receive a maximum award of $35,000 per year of 25% of total debt, <u>whichever is smaller</u>.

Tax Consequences. These payments are exempt from state and federal income taxes. $35,000 is the taxable equivalent of $50,000 (assuming a 30% tax bracket).

Time Commitment. Commit to service obligation of at least two years. One year extension may be awarded for up to three additional years, for a maximum service obligation of five years.

Native American Forgiveness Programs

Besides working for a private non-profit practice or a larger public entity or HMO, some physicians may want to consider another alternative- working with Native American Tribes.
You can learn more by going to: www.ihs.gov/loanrepayment/

Who? Applicants are physicians specializing in obstetrics/gynecology, psychiatry, internal medicine, family medicine, and pediatrics.

Requirements. Must serve at a location on a reservation or other specified place by IHS. A few quirks to be aware of: IHS utilizes a ranking system to address the goal of filling staff vacancies in Indian health programs when granting LRP awards. This system assigns priority consideration to Indian health program sites with the greatest staffing needs in specific health profession disciplines. Also, IHS gives priority to applications of American Indians and Alaska Natives and to individuals recruited through the efforts of Indian Tribes and Tribal or Indian organizations.

The Nitty Gritty Payment Details. Physicians are eligible to receive up to $20,000 per year in health professions educational loan repayment when working for the IHS.

Tax Consequences. <u>These payments are subject to state and federal income taxes</u>. IHS will pay an additional 20% to the IRS to offset increased tax liability.

Time Commitment. A two-year service commitment is required.

National Health Service Corps Loan Repayment Program

In addition to the state programs, there are various other granting national programs and opportunities. For example, the NHSC Loan Repayment program provides loan repayment assistance to licensed medical providers who serve in communities with limited access to health care. There are both full-time and half-time options for service commitment. The dollar amount of assistance and length of service depend on participation in either the full- or half-time and on the need on the Health Professional Shortage Area (HPSA) score of the site.

Essentially, they are looking to fill physicians in "underserved" areas across the country. If you have one right in your area, this could be your ticket!

You can learn more about this program by going here: http://nhsc.hrsa.gov/loanrepayment/

Who? Selection is based on the staffing needs of the NHSC. For physicians, priority for selection will be given to those who have completed residencies in the following: family medicine, obstetrics/gynecology, pediatrics, psychiatry, geriatrics, or internal medicine.

Requirements. In exchange for loan repayment, participants are obligated to serve full-time upon completion of training at a designated NHSC-LRP site of their choice. US Citizenship required.

The Nitty Gritty Payment Details. Physicians may receive repayment of up to $50,000 in health professions educational loans (depending on site). Primary care providers working full-time at an NHSC-approved site with a HPSA score of 14 or above can receive up to $50,000 in loan repayment for committing to serve at site for at least two years.

Primary care providers working full-time at an NHSC-approved site with a HPSA score of 13 or below can receive up to $30,000 in loan repayment for committing to serve at the site for at least two years.

Tax Consequences. The loan repayments are exempt from gross income and employment taxes. These funds are not included as wages when determining benefits under the Social Security Act.

Time Commitment. It is a minimum of two years, but the physician could choose to stay longer. At the end of two years, Corps members can apply to continue their service and receive additional loan repayment. With continued service, providers may be able to pay off all their student loans!

What If….. I Don't Want (or can't do) A Debt Forgiveness Program?

Learn How To Slash Your Interest Rate In Half!

You may be wondering… *what if I don't work for a non-profit?*

You may be wondering… *why couldn't I just pay off my debt quicker on my own?*

When the banks were thrown into the pits in the depths of the debt crisis, we've seen a tremendous change in the way student loans have operated.

Practically every single resident or fellow is paying somewhere between 6% and 7% in interest rate. On $200,000 worth of debt, we're talking about $13,000 a year in interest or nearly $1,000 a month!

If you think about virtually any loan, like a mortgage or a car loan, if you have a high interest rate today and tomorrow interest rates drop, you could get it refinanced somewhere. Your 6% loan can become a

5% loan.

Yet, for student loans, there became this vacuum. You couldn't get them refinanced. Docs have been stuck with these crazy high interest rates even though the Fed has driven interest rates to be crazy crazy low. And we couldn't make it happen!

In this void, private equity & some small banks have started to step-in and is making refinancing possible today for many physicians.

SoFi (Social Finance) backed by private equity investors became one of the early entrants into this space.

In a recent podcast on DoctorFreedomPodcast.com, founder Dan Macklin said, "I was at Stanford Business School… it's one of the best business schools in the country. These are very smart people, very employable people, but we saw that our classmates were paying really, really high rates for their loans. First, a lot of people were borrowing and secondly, they were paying ridiculously high rates for their loans, six, seven, eight percent. We thought it was strange that once you graduated you couldn't then refinance that debt."

Today, SoFi specializes in refinancing loans AFTER a physician has transitioned to practice. They currently do NOT have a program while a physician is in residency.

Most physicians are paying 6%, 7%, or even 8%. SoFi's rates have varied as low as 3.5% on a fixed rate and on 1.9% on a variable rate.

Physicians could save 2%, 3%, 4%, or 5% and slash their cost in half and as result saving tens of thousands of dollars in the process.

The interest rates quoted by SoFi can be different from physician to physician. Dan Macklin noted that, "There's no exact debt-income ratio that we're looking for. There isn't a perfect number that I can tell you… it's slightly different for everybody because we look at a number of things including the credit history, what school you went to, what kind of profession you're doing, where you major, etc but among those things the salary is very important."

The amazing this is that regardless of who you choose- whether it is SoFi or DRB or another company, there is NO cost to doing a refinancing. With mortgages, I usually think of mortgage refinancing and points. There are NO origination fees, refinancing costs, or points currently with the loan refinancers. There's also no repayment penalty. So, you could pay back your loans earlier if you desired to.

How many people can qualify with SoFi's lowest interest rate?

Dan Macklin said, "It's pretty much a bell shaped curve in terms of our rates. So, if I take out five year rate… it goes from 1.9% to 4.1%. The average person that gets approved by SoFi somewhere in the middle…. physicians [are] among the kind of a demographic who many of them get that highest rate, not everybody gets there of course but a very, very high number of people do get it."

You can get a $250 refinancing bonus by going to SoFi.com/250 to refinance your loans with SoFi.

Another company that specializes in refinancing medical student loans is Darien Rowayton Bank (DRB). They started a little bit later in the debt refinancing game than SoFi, but are aggressively moving into their territory.

DRB has very similar interest rates and offers. However, they did note in a recent interview on DoctorFreedomPodcast.com that they DO NOT utilize their rates on a bell shaped curve and instead tend to offer lower competitive rates with many physicians.

In addition, they recently launched a program that residents can refinance their loans WHILE in residency or fellowship. This is completely new & unique to the marketplace.

DRB has tried to model the Public Service Loan Forgiveness Program (PSLF) and income-based repayment program (IBR) as closely as possible by limiting the maximum monthly payment to $100/mo while in residency.

In the meantime, with interest rates getting locked in at historic rates, your interest is accruing at likely half of what the used to be. Rather than a $1,000 a month, you may only be owing $400 or $500 a month.

This is tremendous when you consider the value of compounding!

The bummer is that you can NO LONGER participate in PSLF. No debt forgiveness, only debt pay-off that you create for yourself!

However, you'll be in control of your own destiny rather than relying on the government which is worth considering.

The Ophthalmologist

In 2012, my partner Roger and I met a young ophthalmologist and his lovely wife. They had several young kids and another on the way.

They were buried underneath $200,000 worth of student loans and he was transitioning to practice within only a few months.

They wanted to buy a home and save for their kids' college education. How could they balance all these different desires?

Together, we worked through a number of different scenarios and found that IBR was the best format for them. We even identified which loans to pay off first.

Fast forward a few years later- he is now in private practice. Thus, he was no longer eligible for debt forgiveness. We switched gears and now they are on track to refinance their debts and slash the interest in half.

They are now happily settled, enjoying life, and not worrying about their debt, because they have a plan of action.

Final Thoughts

As a physician, you've made a commitment to helping others and your community.

Now make a plan to pay-off your debt!

Consider for a moment… could you utilize one of the programs we have discussed?

Also, one other topic this isn't discussed enough, what if you could COMBINE two of these programs simultaneously?

For example, you could enroll in PSLF, work for a non-profit in an under-served area, and then at the SAME TIME, do a state forgiveness program for 2 or 3 or 4 years (whatever the minimum commitment is).

5 Steps To Get Out of Debt Action Guide for Physicians

This could hedge the bet of the federal government taking away the punch bowl from the party. This way you have substantially less debt no matter what happens.

If, as a young physician, you focus on paying off your debts, save for a rainy day, live within your means and put money away for retirement, you can then do the things you've long dreamed of doing and be well down the road to financial independence.

Take the next step and complete the action steps on the next page!

2.1 **Action Step:** Gather together the data that you will need for all of your liabilities.

We'll cover how to prioritize liabilities in step three, but for right now just get the information.

Below we have included an example for your review.

Liability Descrip.	Company	Principal Owed	Interest Rate	Maturity Date	Minimum Payment	Current Payment	House, Consumer, Or Business?	Fixed or Variable?	If VA, when change?
Home Mortgage	Bank of America	$ 250,000	4.50%	1/1/2032	$ 1,400	$ 1,400	House	Fixed	
HELOC	Bank of America	$ 10,000	2.50%	n/a	$ 21	$ 21	House	Variable	Monthly
Student Loan	Sallie Mae	$ 150,000	6.80%	1/1/2033	$ 1,000	$ 1,000	Consum	Fixed	
Car Loan	BECU	$ 10,000	5.00%	1/1/2017	$ 300	$ 350	Consum	Fixed	
Credit Card	Bank of America	$ 30,000	11.00%	n/a	$ 125	$ 150	Business	Variable	Annually

Note how nearly every spot has something in it.

Of course, fixed loans don't have anything in the final column since it is only for variable loans.

I entered in "n/a" for maturity date for the lines of credit since there is no definite maturity date.

One of our goals will be to make a specific maturity date once we have identified the loans that are a priority.

Below is a template for you to complete.

5 Steps To Get Out of Debt Action Guide for Physicians

If you are confused by this process or need help getting the information together, feel free to give me a call or send me an e-mail.

Liability Description	Company	Principal Owed	Interest Rate	Maturity Date	Minimum Payment	Current Payment	House, Consumer, Or Business?	Fixed or Variable?	If VA, when change?

For more information, go to www.daviddenniston.com/physicians or www.DoctorFreedomPodcast.com.
For questions, e-mail: dave@daviddenniston.com
Or call 800-548-1820

5 Steps To Get Out of Debt Action Guide for Physicians

Now that you have defined your reality, take some time to reflect on how you've gotten this point.

2.2 Action Step: What positive things have I done to put myself in a <u>healthy</u> financial position?

_____
_____
_____
_____
_____

2.3 Action Step: What are some areas I have sabotaged myself? <u>Where can I improve</u>?

_____
_____
_____
_____
_____

2.4 Action Step: Who are some positive mentors/rolemodels that can help hold me accountable to my goal of becoming debt free? Speak with that mentor and make a schedule of meeting with them at least twice a year, if not quarterly.

_____
_____
_____
_____
_____

For more information, go to www.daviddenniston.com/physicians or www.DoctorFreedomPodcast.com.
For questions, e-mail: dave@daviddenniston.com
Or call 800-548-1820

2.5 Action Step: Review over ALL of the debt strategies listed throughout the last 10 pages. Could you utilize a debt-forgiveness program? Is PSLF a good fit? Are you married? Should you consider a strategy like married filing separately? Should you consider a state sponsored program?

Could you COMBINE PSLF with a state sponsored program to hedge your bets?

If you are not going to work for a non-profit, could you refinance your debt through a company like SoFi or DRB? Are you willing to make a commitment to working in the for-profit arena as a resident? Could you refinance your debt while you are still in residency?

Write down your thoughts below.

_____
_____
_____
_____
_____
_____
_____
_____
_____
_____

5 Steps To Get Out of Debt Action Guide for Physicians

STEP three | Define Your Roadmap/Goals

Now that we have made your financial reality visible, we have a blank canvas- a map. We know the names of the cities and the states you are going to travel to. Next, we need to figure out how you are going to get there. What are the roads and freeways you need to take to travel there?

It all starts with one basic question, "What is a tangible goal you have that requires money and planning to achieve?"

Dream big! Keep realistic, but allow your mind to wander and think of the possibilities. Paint the picture of what your life would look like as you achieve this goal and afterwards.

The answer should come in three different parts:

1) What is the goal?   2) How much money will it take?   3) By when will you achieve it?

After filling in your answer, take some time to reflect and think about how you will feel once you have achieved your goal.

Below we have shown an example road sign. Then we have included a page of 'road signs' for you to fill in.

Goal: Pay off student loans.

Amount: $150,000

- Currently matures 1/1/2032
- Paying $1,400/mo

Achieve By: 1/1/2025

Give Two or Three Feelings or Thoughts on How You Would Feel for Achieving this Goal

_____

<u>Amazed! Elated! It would feel awesome!</u>

<u>Can I retire now?</u>

_____

For more information, go to www.daviddenniston.com/physicians or www.DoctorFreedomPodcast.com.
For questions, e-mail: dave@daviddenniston.com
Or call 800-548-1820

The Orthopedic Surgeon & The ER Doctor

I find that there are two different kinds of people in the world. Those who enjoy sharing their feelings and being introspective, and those who don't.

I went through this exercise with one of my clients, an orthopedic surgeon and his wife. We talked for about 30 minutes on what was important to them, getting down to the nitty gritty and what really motivates their life. We then moved onto the same goal exercise described on previous page. They loved it! They were able to talk out their goals in a way they had never thought of before. It helped them to see reality and the possibilities.

As a matter of fact, they told me it was the best conversation they ever had!

Then, there are those on the opposite side of the table. I had an E.R. doctor once review Version 1.0 of this workbook, and his reaction was less than stellar to doing this kind of exercise. He said something to the effect of, "This touchy-feely stuff isn't for me!"

However, I would encourage you to give it a go—ESPECIALLY if you are married. Talk to your spouse and go through it together!

5 Steps To Get Out of Debt Action Guide for Physicians

3.1 Action Step: Write down two of your tangible goals that require money and planning to achieve. Then, take a step back. Reflect for a minute on what it would be like to get there. Give two or three feelings/thoughts on how you would feel after achieving this goal. Feel free to print out this page multiple times if you have many goals.

Goal:

Amount:

Achieve By:

Give Two or Three Feelings or Thoughts on How You Would Feel for Achieving this Goal

_____

_____

_____

Goal:

Amount

Achieve By:

Give Two or Three Feelings or Thoughts on How You Would Feel for Achieving this Goal

_____

_____

_____

For more information, go to www.daviddenniston.com/physicians or www.DoctorFreedomPodcast.com.
For questions, e-mail: dave@daviddenniston.com
Or call 800-548-1820

STEP Four | How to Determine Priorities & Payoff Decisions

By now, you have made a balance sheet for yourself- including all of your assets and liabilities. Also, you have also established the framework for your tangible goals and when you want to achieve them.

Here are a few basic ideas to consider in determining your priorities:

In general, look to pay off highest interest rate, lowest balance consumer debts first.

Specifically, eliminate consumer debts including credit cards, car loans, and student loans. None of these are tax deductible like a mortgage or a HELOC (assuming over 130k AGI). If possible, move consumer debts to tax deductible debt like a mortgage, assuming that you feel comfortable with your income on a go-forward basis.

If interest costs are 3% difference or more, go after the largest interest rates. If less than 3% difference and 5 years or less to maturity, consider paying off the lowest balance loan.

Outside of making sure to meet minimum payments, put any "above and beyond" payments of additional principal all towards only ONE loan so that you can demolish it quickly.

Let's take some action steps to customize these ideas to your specific situation. The next logical step we need to take is reviewing over the data from previous exercises and consider the prioritization of how to address the liabilities.

4.1 Action Step: Have you recently graduated from medical school or you are early in your residency?

Review over Step 2 when I discussed either deferring your loan (where interest will compound) or forbearing through programs such as an income-sensitive repayment plan (IBR) or pay-as-you-earn repayment plan (PER).

5 Steps To Get Out of Debt Action Guide for Physicians

IBR and PER are both great in situations where you may be considering loan forgiveness programs. PER requires you to pay less on a monthly basis and may be a better fit for your situation.

Also, sign up for an auto-withdrawal if the lender offers a slight interest rate deduction.

4.2 Action Step: Are you a year or two from entering into full-time practice? As we discussed earlier, consider debt-forgiveness programs that are available through potential employers, federal, or state sources.

Check out…

http://studentaid.ed.gov/repay-loans/forgiveness-cancellation/charts/public-service

https://services.aamc.org/fed_loan_pub/

http://NHSC.hrsa.gov/loanrepayment/studentstoserviceprogram/.

4.3 Action Step: Review over Action Step 2.1(liabilities). Get a red (or pink) highlighter, a yellow highlighter, a green highlighter, and a blue highlighter.

4.4 Action Step: ONLY in the "fixed or variable column", highlight all <u>variable</u> debts in red (or pink).

4.5 Action Step: ONLY in the "interest" column, highlight your 3 HIGHEST interest rate debts in yellow.

4.6 Action step: ONLY in the "principal" column, highlight your three LOWEST principal balances in green.

4.7 Action step: ONLY in the "monthly payment" columns, highlight your three HIGHEST monthly payments in blue.

4.8 Action step: Take a look at what you have highlighted so far on each row. Are you seeing any trends develop? Does any one particular row have multiple highlights? Write your thoughts down below.

_____

_____

_____

4.9 Action step: Think for a few moments about your primary objectives. Are you more interested in increasing cash flow or lowering your interest costs? If cash flow, consider first eliminating liabilities that have the lowest principal balance. Alternatively, if interest rates are significantly higher and lowering your interest costs is more important, consider eliminating those liabilities first. Write a few thoughts down below.

_____

_____

_____

4.10 Action step: Interest rates could rise in the next few years and variable debts could become a tremendous problem for many folks. In the margins of the table from Action Step 2.1, number the <u>variable</u> debts in order from largest principal balance to the smallest. Think about the consequences if interest rates rise by 1% or 2%. For example, a $20,000 loan has little consequence- $200 to $400 interest annually whereas a $100,000 loan has much more severe consequences- $1,000 to $2,000 annually.

4.11 Action step: Based on the three previous action steps, designate one debt to be your 'top priority debt'. Then, designate the second most important debt to be your "next priority debt".

My Top Priority Debt Is: _____

My Next Priority Debt Is: _____

4.12 Action step: Compare your producing assets to your liabilities. Between liquid assets and non-qualified money, consider having a total cash cushion of 6 months to 1 year worth of living expenses. Beyond that cushion, utilize the excess funds to pay down your 'top priority debt'.

4.13 Action step: Focus on paying off one debt through extra payments. This should increase your cash flow more quickly.

Use the "Loan Pay-Off Calculator" spreadsheet that we have on our website to determine how quickly you can actually pay off the "priority debt".

Then, based off of the date you establish, figure out how quickly you can pay off the second debt.

<u>After</u> you pay-off the first debt, consider splitting the additional cash flow between your "next priority debt" and non-qualified savings.

4.14 Action step: Review over Action Step 3.1 and consider revising your tangible goal 'road signs'. Feel free to print additional copies of Action Step 3.1 in order to re-assess and update your success..

4.15 Action step: Take some time to reflect on what you've just done. How do you feel?

Making a plan is a fantastic way to get started. It is a beginning!

However, it's implementing that allows you to get the results. Just like thinking about exercise won't make you physically fit- write down your commitment to implement your plan and what you will do to stay on track. Show your plan to your mentor. Brainstorm with them- what can you do to avoid financial distractions and pitfalls?

_____

_____

_____

_____

STEP five | What Do I Spend Monthly & Where Can I Improve?

The final step in our journey is to discover and strategize how much you can put towards debt without substantially changing your lifestyle. This can be very time intensive if you want to understand every nut and bolt on a weekly basis. However, it can also be pretty straight-forward and easy to do if you want to look only on a monthly or bi-monthly basis.

5.1 Action step: Buy or sign up for a cash flow/spending tracking software programs. Common examples include Mint.com, Quicken, MVelopes, and countless others. We use EMoney Advisor. For any resident or fellow, we provide this software for free. For a quick overview of this program, check out:

http://www.emoneyadvisor.com/emacorp/video.aspx?vid=box&w=853&h=480&lang=en

Some are free and other cost money. Some banks and credit cards offer some software as well. Explore one or two of these programs.

5 Steps To Get Out of Debt Action Guide for Physicians

Choose one and sign up for it.

5.2 Action step: Link in all of your assets and liabilities through the service you selected. This typically involves log-ins through the financial sources that you use.

5.3 Action step: The best programs will automatically categorize your expenses. It may not be entirely correct. Consider looking through the activity or correcting the categories.

Common examples that usually need categorizing include checks that are written, mom & pop stores, and small restaurants.

5.4 Action step: In the software, Go to the section that puts your monthly spending all together. For example, in E-Money Advisor, the 'Trends' tab. Fill in these charts...

My Monthly Spending:

This Month	Previous Month	Two Months Ago	Three Months Ago

My Biggest 4 Expense Categories

This Month	Previous Month	Two Months Ago	Three Months Ago
1.	1.	1.	1.
2.	2.	2.	2.
3.	3.	3.	3.
4.	4.	4.	4.

5.5 Action step: As you look at the data above, find two of three ways that you can lower your monthly expense. Perhaps, consider shopping for lower cost medical/auto/home insurance. See if you can refinance your mortgage. Cut out a trip to Starbucks, eat out less often, take lunch to work more often, etc, etc. Write them down below:

_____

_____

_____

5.6 Action step: Now that we've talked about expenses. The next logical step is to think about ways to increase your income. If you've increased your income and decreased your expenses, you are well on your way on the path to financial prosperity!

How have you increased your income in the past? How can you increase your income in the future?

_____

_____

_____

What training or additional education or certification may allow you to gain a promotion at work or more desirable to other employers or clients?

_____

_____

_____

Consider starting your own small business or moonlighting. Many people today sell trinkets or hobbies through E-Bay or Amazon.com. What are your talents? What are your passions?

Alternatively, check out FreelancePhysician.com for moonlighting opportunities for physicians. You can get paid $150/hour or more. One of my physician friends is now making more money from moonlighting than from his full-time job. What opportunities could be available to you?

_____

_____

_____

Final Thoughts

Congratulations! You've just accomplished something that very few people have every done in their lives.

You have taken the time to invest into your future. You have made a balance sheet- identifying your assets and liabilities. You have established goals with specific dates. You've even targeted two specific debts that you are going to eliminate. Just as importantly, you've also set up some tools to help monitor your spending as well as to increase your income.

Take the next step- implement those promises you made to yourself.

We cannot control so many things in our lives- the weather, your favorite sports team winning the big game, being sick, a family member passing away, children that make poor decisions, and so much more.

However, your debt and how you treat them **are in your power**. Take control today. Live within your means. You can do it!

I encourage you to revisit this workbook on an annual basis. I will make updates based on your feedback. So, please let me know your experience and where I can improve.

If you would like any additional support and to learn more about how I can serve you, please feel free to contact me anytime at dave@daviddenniston.com or call me at (800) 548-1890.

Let's take this journey together and get you on the path to financial freedom.

Warm Regards,

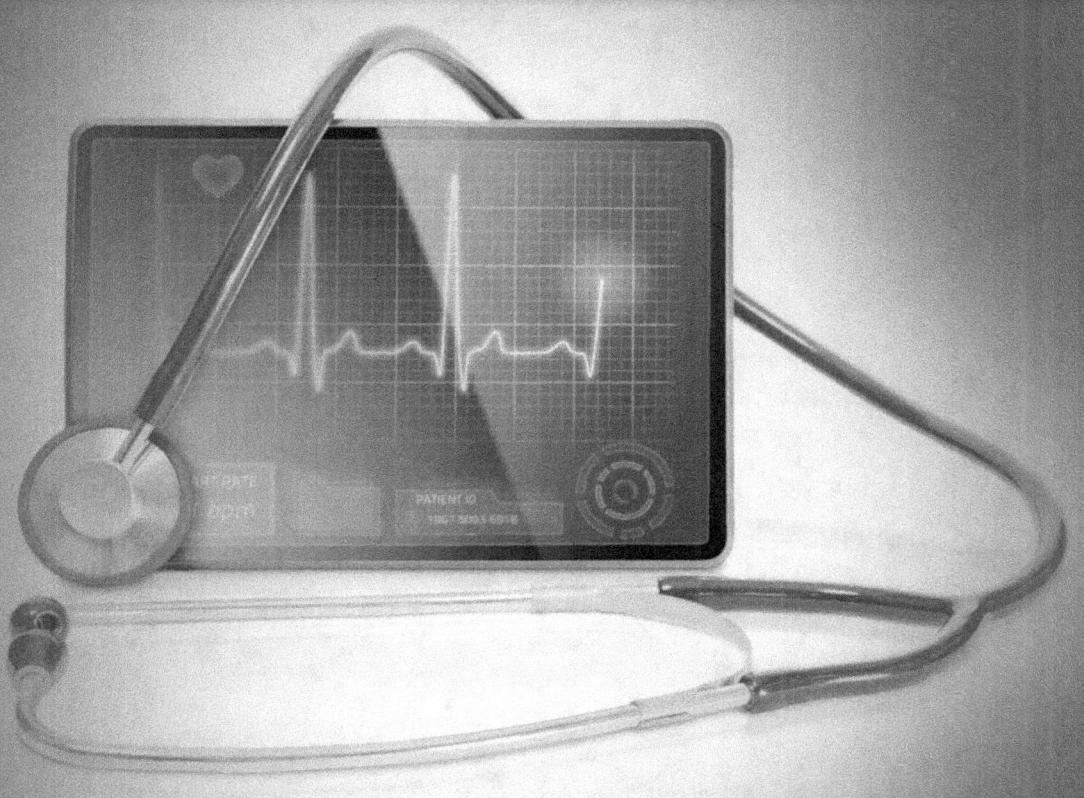

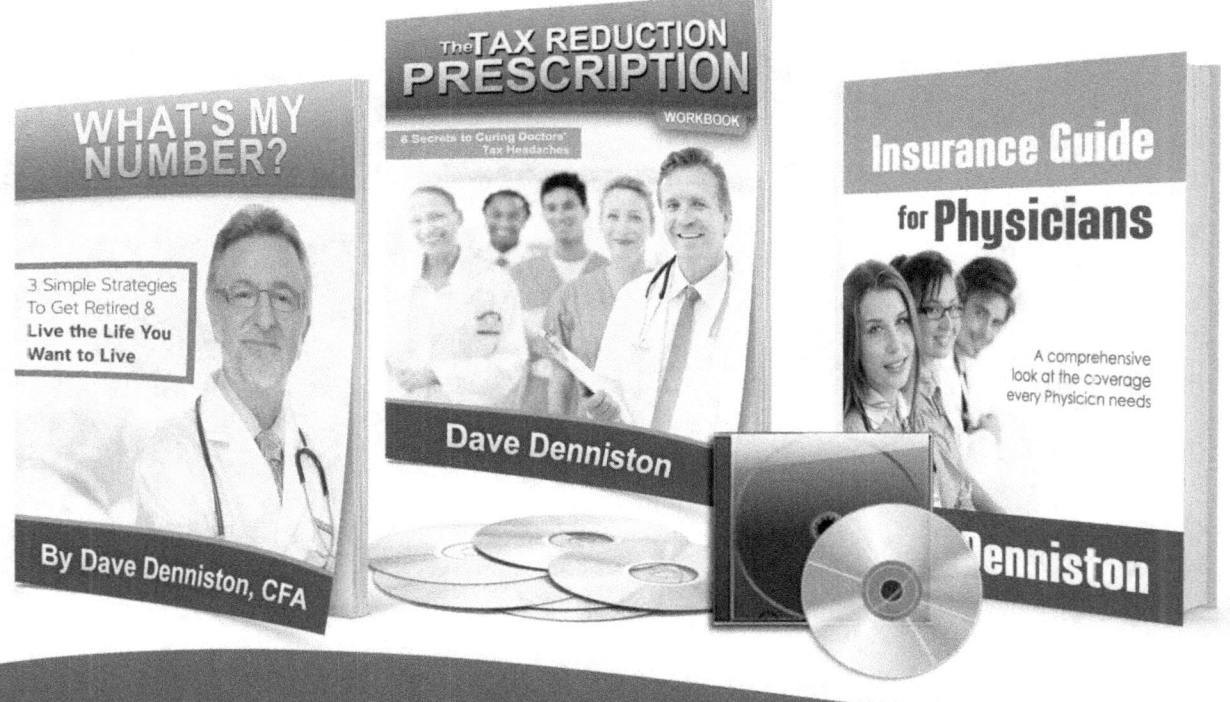

www.ingramcontent.com/pod-product-compliance
Lightning Source LLC
Chambersburg PA
CBHW081753170526
45167CB00009B/4016